30 Day Guided Prophetic Journal

Becky King

Foreword by Dan McCollam

Copyright © 2015 Becky King
All rights reserved. This book, or parts thereof, may not be reproduced in any form without permission from the author
Scripture quotations taken from the New American Standard Bible®,
Copyright © 1960, 1962, 1963, 1968, 1971, 1972, 1973, 1975, 1977, 1995 by The Lockman Foundation
Used by permission." (www.Lockman.org)

Cover photo and design by Shelby Gibbs
You can find more of her work at
http://www.thegildedhive.com

ISBN: 1507711484
ISBN-13: 978-1507711484

ACKNOWLEDGEMENTS

My niece Emily, the day you were born renewed in me the importance of seeking the Lord for the future. To ask, pray, love, and co-create a better world for the next generation to live in.

Mom, no words can express the depths of my love for you. You are my hero. Thank you for always believing in me.

Mission Church Vacaville, Believer's Church Tulsa, and Tulsa House church families, you are gifts from God and have brought such riches to my life. I will love you forever and ever.

Shelby Gibbs, Patricia & Larry Domansky, thank you for contributing your editing skills, graphic design talents, wise council, and patience to make this book complete. I couldn't have done it without you.

Last but not least: Dan McCollam, thank you for pushing me over the cliff.

FORWARD

Why Prophetic Journaling?

How blessed we are to live in a day with such strong and free prophetic grace and unction. Before our very eyes, we are seeing God's dream fulfilled as sons and daughters prophesy through the generous outpouring of the Holy Spirit. Believers, who are comfortable hearing and speaking the thoughts and heart of God through prophecy, seem to be hungering for another level.

There are many keys to unlocking and stepping into the next levels of prophetic grace that will continue to be revealed in this and the next generation. Prophetic journaling is one of those keys.

In Habakkuk chapter two, God is training a young prophet. The prophet commits himself to watch before the Lord for a prophetic word and wisdom saying, "I will stand at my watch and station myself on the ramparts; I will look to see what he will say to me, and what answer I am to give to this complaint." God answers the young prophet by asking him to journal what he is hearing. "Then the Lord replied, 'Write down the revelation and make it plain on tablets so that a herald may run with it. For the revelation awaits an appointed time; it speaks of the end and will not prove false.

Though it linger, wait for it; it will certainly come and will not delay.'" (Habakkuk 2:1-3)

Prophetic journaling facilitates the strengths of both an inward and outward processor. As we think through the words, images, and prophetic feelings, we must find language that conveys the heart and weight of the message. This is a powerful form of inward processing. Then as we see the words on the page and meditate over their deeper meaning, we also have the opportunity to enjoy the potent force of outward, external processing. In this way, we are being careful stewards of the prophetic grace we have been given.

Prophetic journaling also helps believers be responsible for their own personal development. Scripture commands us, "Train yourself to be godly." (1 Timothy 4:7) The original Greek that much of the New Testament was written in uses the word "gymnazo" much like our word "gymnasium." It not only has a similar sound but also a similar meaning. In modern vernacular, we might say, "Take your spirituality to the gym and give it a work out." Don't wait for supernatural things to someday pop out of the air. Go after them in training your ear, your heart, your sensitivities, and your faith. Journaling helps us track how faithful we have been in stationing ourselves to listen for the voice of God.

I'm thankful that Becky King, a friend and student of the prophetic, has put together this helpful prophetic journaling tool from her own experiences. She is an emerging prophetess, who is contributing to a great local and global prophetic company. My prayer is that those that are hungry for a next-level experience in the prophetic will use tools like these to sharpen their gifts and press further into the riches of His grace, poured out so lavishly on His sons and daughters.

Stay faithful to your watch. Write out your prophetic impressions. Sharpen them with an ever increasing knowledge of the word and through the intimacy of prayer. Commit to a community that runs with the word of the Lord. Wait with joyful expectation and hold fast to humility, accountability, and teachability. In this way, you will honor the grace that we are currently enjoying while enlarging our capacities for an even more glorious future.

God bless your journey,
Dano

Dan McCollam is the founding director of Mission School of Prophecy, co-founder of Bethel School of the Prophets, and author of <u>Basic Training in Prophetic Activation</u>. Dan also serves as part of the core leadership team at The Mission in Vacaville, CA.

INTRODUCTION

Several years ago at the advice of a mentor, I started keeping a journal specifically for prophetic words and things I was seeing in the Spirit. As I started this journey, I questioned whether journaling was biblical; and as a tool, would it help me grow as a prophet? The answer to my first question was as simple as opening up the Bible. There I discovered God's instructions "to write" were everywhere.

For example, in Isaiah 8:1, the Lord told Isaiah, "Now go, write it on a tablet before them and inscribe it on a scroll, that it may serve in the time to come as a witness forever." Also in Jeremiah 30:2, we find "Thus says the LORD, the God of Israel, 'Write all the words which I have spoken to you in a book.'" Then in Jeremiah 36:28, he is told to rewrite that which had been lost. "Take again another scroll and write on it all the former words that were on the first scroll which Jehoiakim the king of Judah burned." In Habakkuk 2:2, he is told to record the vision the Lord has given him. Similarly, in Revelation 1:19, John is instructed to write what he sees in his vision.

If the prophets had not been obedient to write their visions and dreams, there would have been no written record to help prepare and guide Israel and future generations. There would be no written testimony of the hope of the coming Christ, the outpouring the Holy Spirit, or the fulfillment of God's dream to restore our relationship with Him.

As I journaled, I quickly discovered its value as my prophetic gift was increasing. On this journey, I learned that the Lord wanted to share even the tiniest of details with me. Asking questions and crying out for more was not only allowed but was part of the pursuit of stewarding my prophetic gift. Paul says it best, "Do not neglect the spiritual gift within you, which was bestowed on you through prophetic utterance with the laying on of hands by the presbytery. Take pains with these things; be absorbed in them, so that your progress will be evident to all." (1 Timothy 4:14-15)

Clearly, it is our responsibility to steward and train ourselves in our gifts. Since Pentecost, we are living in a time that is characterized by the voice of God. With the outpouring of Holy Spirit, prophecy and the other gifts have been operating in God's people all over the world. Yet, there is a depth that is still available to be explored. In this season, we are being calling to grow like Jesus in wisdom and in favor with God and with man. (Luke 2:52) The Lord is looking for people who He can trust and place in positions of influence, prophetic voices that can discern when to declare or hold a word, and saints that can destroy the works of the enemy and co-create a hope and a future. There is no limit in the ways in which Holy Spirit will reveal and teach us new things if we are willing to step out in faith.

I hope that as you take this journey, you too will experience an upgrade in your prophetic gift. Like Paul, "I pray that the eyes of your heart may be enlightened, so that you will know what is the hope of His calling, what are the riches of the glory of His inheritance in the saints." (Ephesians 1:18) May Holy Spirit lead and guide you through this adventure.

Blessings to you on this journey,

Becky King

HOW TO USE THIS JOURNAL

"Call to Me and I will answer you, and I will tell you great and mighty things, which you do not know." (Jeremiah 33:3)

What a promise! As your start to practice prophetic journaling, ask the Lord to speak to you. Jeremiah 33:3 declares He will. Journaling is a great tool to build your confidence and exercise your gift. Here are some ways in which journaling can contribute to your development.

- You get more revelation when you journal. As you write, you become more aware of His voice and what He is saying.

- It provides a safe place to practice receiving and processing prophetic revelation without the pressure of public exposure.

- Journaling helps you understand what God is saying so that you can communicate it in a simple yet powerful way.

- Prophetic journaling gives you the opportunity to co-create with God to see things Holy Spirit has shared come to pass.

- Your discernment in the prophetic will grow as you learn what to share, what to hold in prayer, and what to declare.

- You are building a history of what The Lord has spoken to you that you can reference and judge as time passes.

As you start your journey, this book will serve as a guide. Each day will consist of a writing exercise. These journaling methods are tools not rules. This is ultimately about your journey with Holy Spirit so don't be afraid to write how and where He leads you.

One of the most important things to remember when you are journaling is that your entries should always line up with the guidelines of biblical New Testament prophecy. Look for the gold in people and situations. Are your words encouraging, and uplifting? Look for pathways to reconciliation, restoration, or healing?

Your journal is a private and a safe way for you to explore how and what the Lord is speaking. You don't need to share every part of it; but when you do receive a word that you think you need to share or bring to light, get some accountability and judgment of the word first. What you write in a prophetic journal is still subject to the biblically mandated process for the prophetic. (1 Cor 14:29, 1 Cor 13:9,12)

Accountability of your prophetic journaling is not limited too but can include submitting to leadership and mentors, checking against biblical principles, and keeping a record of accuracy over time.

From time to time, what the Lord shares with you might be plans of the enemy or a situation that need redemption. Seeing and documenting things of that nature are not to be feared. However, in those situations, press in for more. Ask how you should respond or pray for these issues to be resolved in a positive way. Being prophetic is just as much about stopping the enemy's advancement as it is about furthering the gospel. Remember love is always our greatest weapon.

Day One
Free Write

Free write is a technique in which a person writes continuously without regard to spelling, grammar, or topic. It may seem to lack structure or sense, but it helps writers overcome blocks of apathy and self-criticism.

Say a short prayer, asking the Lord what He would like to share with you today then start writing. Don't wait until you hear the answer or topic; simply write anything that comes to mind. Even if what comes to your mind doesn't make sense, keep writing. When you are done, read back over what you have written. You might be surprised with the results.

Today's goal is to get used to writing.

Example: Here I am writing. Not really sure what I want to write about, but I'm sure something will come to mind. We could really use some rain. I want rain! I want to feel cozy inside, with my candles lit and reading a book or watching a movie under a blanket while the pitter patter of rain comes down. I would watch it out the window and smile as I sipped tea. I wonder if the flowers wish for rain. Rain can be so refreshing. I love it when it is warm enough outside to play in the rain.

"You will succeed in whatever you choose to do, and light will shine on the road ahead of you."
Job 22:28

"Being willing to do what you are not qualified to do is sometimes what qualifies you." Bill Johnson

Day Two
Bullet Points

Make a list of personal things in which you want to hear from the Lord. Once you have your list go back and write a short phrase of what you feel Holy Spirit is saying concerning each item. Make a commitment to pray and ask for more wisdom on these issues throughout the day. We will do more with this list tomorrow.

Today's goal is to learn that our writing does not have to be long and detailed for it to be significant.

Example:

1. Family - Set your priorities

2. Promotion - The path before me is laid out

3. Finance - Do not give up sowing

"Ask, and it will be given to you; seek, and you will find; knock, and it will be opened to you."
Matthew 7:7

"The simple things done consistently will produce the greatest results in your life." Doug Addison

Day Three
Bullet Point Follow-Up

Write a prophetic word for the items you listed yesterday. Come back to this entry over the next few days and declare the word into the atmosphere. If you want to go a step further, you can revisit this entry in a few weeks and document if you have seen what you prophesied come to pass in your life.

Today's goal is to go back to a topic and ask the Lord for more details and information and see that He will respond.

Example: As you step into a new place of promotion, the Lord has prepared the path for you. He goes before you. He is with you in this journey and He declares you are worthy of the blessings coming to you. You have been faithful to your family. Your prayers for them are heard in the halls of Heaven and they are not forgotten. You have sown, and now it is a season of reaping. However, don't give up in sowing again. You are a giver and have a heart to bless the people around you out of your abundance.

"Pursue love, yet eagerly desire spiritual gifts, but especially that you may prophesy." 1 Corinthians 14:1

"You are co-seated with Christ in Heavenly places. Go deep, and live from Heaven!" Georgian Banov

Day Four
SOAP Method
(Scripture, Observation, Application, Prayer)

Use the scripture Jeremiah 33:3. After you have meditated on this verse for a bit, journal about the promise in this verse and how it relates to prophecy? What does it say about God's willingness to share with us? Rewrite the verse as a declaration over yourself that you can and are hearing from God

Today's goal is to incorporate scripture into your prophetic journaling.

Example: This is normal SOAP, but feel free to simply write a paragraph or more with your revelations.

Scripture: "I can do all things through Christ who strengthens me" Philippians 4:13

Observation: There is nothing that I can't do with Christ living in me because He gives me strength for anything that comes my way.

Application: I need to remember that the Word of God does not lie, and it says that I can do ALL things through Christ, and that means *ALL things*!

Prayer: Lord, help me to rely upon your strength. Help me to remember that you promised that I can do anything with your help. Amen.

"Your Word is a lamp to my feet and a light to my feet."
Psalm 119:105

"It takes the Word of God plus the Spirit of God to equal the Truth of God." Kris Vallotton

Day Five
Mind-Mapping

Choose a prophetic biblical character and place their name at the center of the page. Form branches that are quality traits, events, or Bible verses that relate to the character.
How do the things you wrote speak to you in regard to your gift.
Because you don't have to write your idea in any order, it takes the pressure off. You can put down your ideas as you think of them randomly. Be creative.

The goal of today's exercise is to get us thinking and seeing out of the box.

Example:

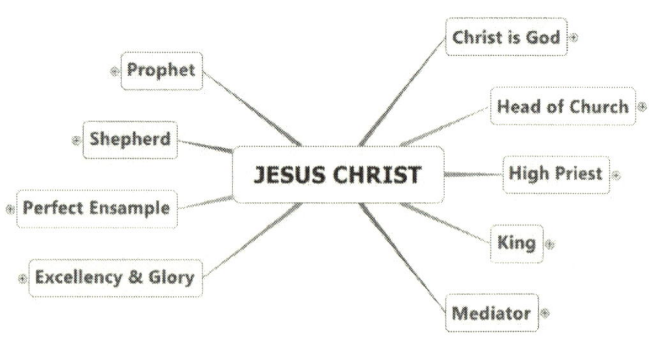

"I press on toward the goal for the prize of the upward call of God in Christ Jesus." Philippians 3:14

"Prophecy is the love language of God." Dan McCollam

Day Six
Prophetic Dream Interpretation

Think of a dream you remember and ask God for prophetic insight. If you don't have a dream you remember, take a few moments now to daydream. This is similar to dream interpretation but might include some strategy on how to respond to the dream.

Today's goal is to learn how to process our dreams from a prophetic standpoint.

Example: In Joseph's dream, he and his brothers were binding sheaves in the field, and his sheaf rose up and stood erect; his brothers sheaves gathered around and bowed down to Joseph's sheaf.

Interpretation could be: One day Joseph would be in a position to be above his brothers. Because it take place in a field, it might be about harvest or food.

"Now may the God of hope fill you with all joy and peace in believing, that you may abound in hope by the power of the Holy Spirit." Romans 15:13

"When we dream with God we have the privilege to co-create masterpieces of his imagination." James Goll

Day Seven
Color and Draw

Today's entry is creative and abstract. Ask Holy Spirit to show you a picture, and then color or draw on this page of your journal. Your drawing doesn't have to be perfect. It could just be some colors on the page. I use stick figures. For this entry, the pages are blank to make it easier to draw.

Today's goal is making a connection between being creative and the prophetic.

EXAMPLE:

"In the beginning God created the heavens and the earth."
Genesis 1:1

"If you seek God's truth, that may now appear dim, out of focus, and distant. it will gradually be revealed." Dieter Uchtdorf

Day Eight
Prophetic Sentence

Compose a short sentence. Ask God to highlight one of the words, and then ask for more understanding of this word. Journal what the Lord is speaking to you.

The goal of today's exercise is to sharpen our attention to detail and learn how to process the details of what we see and hear.

Example: I see angels being dispatched for divine encounters.

Asking Holy Spirit for insight to the word "dispatched" I feel He is saying that angels are ready and waiting for their assignments. Our declarations and prophetic words are those dispatch orders.

"Oh give thanks to the LORD, for He is good;
For His loving kindness is everlasting."
Psalms 106:1

"You may acquire knowledge, but you have to get wisdom from God." Bob Jones

Day Nine
Question and Answer

Think of a question you have about the future, and write it down. Next, record the response you get from the Lord. Once you have His response, ask a follow-up question that will give you more insight. Repeat this question and answer process several times. Ask for details and specific words of knowledge as you go. God will always give us insight, (remember Jeremiah 33:3). There is always more, and scripture tells us He enjoys us asking and seeking out.

Today's goal is to learn that like prayer, the prophetic can be a conversation.

Example:
Me: Lord, what are you doing in my city?

Lord: I am doing a work of establishment. Many saints will be coming into positions of management and ownership.

Me: How will these management and ownership opportunities accomplish the establishment?

Lord: When my people, who are called by my name, step into the positions set before them, the law and economics of the city will shift from operating from a worldly way of thinking to Kingdom wisdom.

"All things came into being through Him, and apart from Him nothing came into being that has come into being."
John 1:3

"Hope is a renewed mindset that looks for positive possibilities in God that might lie ahead." Bob Hartley

Day Ten
Summary and Review

You have the first nine days of prophetic journaling under your belt. Way to go! This is the perfect time to look over your entries from the first section. Highlight and document any things that have come to pass. Then come back and write about how you feel the process is going. Thank God for increase and breakthrough, and share with Him what you hope to get out of the next ten days. The next section will use these daily exercises with a focus on evangelism.

Today is about celebrating your progress.

"Be steadfast, immovable, always abounding in the work of the Lord, knowing that your labor is not in vain."
1 Corinthians 15:58

"It is important to become aware of the impact that your words are having on both others and yourself."
Mark Chironna

Day Eleven
SOAP Method
(Scripture, Observation, Application, Prayer)

Use the scripture 1 Corinthians 13:2. *"If I have the gift of prophecy, and know all mysteries and all knowledge; and if I have all faith, so as to remove mountains, but do not have love, I am nothing."* After you have meditated on this verse for a bit, journal about the verse. What is it speaking to you. How does this verse affect how prophecy should be used when ministering to others, especially pre-Christians?

Today's goal is to remember as prophetic people, love must be the root of all we say and do.

"O give thanks to the Lord, for He is good; for His loving-kindness is everlasting." 1 Chronicles 16:34

"We never grow closer to God when we just live life. It takes deliberate pursuit and attentiveness." Francis Chan

Day Twelve
Prophetic Word Journaling

Think of a person you have been praying for to come to the Lord. Ask for a word for them. Declare and pray over the person and the word, but do not share your word with them`. We will be working with this word for the next few days.

Today's goal is to write a word for the lost that speaks to who they were created to be and their destiny.

"For I know the plans that I have for you,' declares the Lord, plans for welfare and not for calamity to give you a future and a hope." Jeremiah 29:11

"the journey makes things valuable not the title. Learn to enjoy and value the process of what God is doing." Bill Johnson

Day Thirteen
Mind-Mapping

Draw a circle at the center of your page with the name of the person you have word for from yesterday. From there, make branches that are single words or short phrases about the person's good qualities and gifts. Remember this is a prophetic exercise. We are not only listing the good thing we already know about them, we are also asking the Lord for the amazing things He sees about them.

Today's goal is to see the great qualities and gifts the Lord has put in the people around us.

"Being confident of this very thing, That He who begun a good work in you will complete it until the day of Jesus Christ."
Philippians 1:6

"May we be faithful followers of Christ, examples of Righteousness, thus becoming 'lights to the world.'"
Thomas S. Monson

Day Fourteen
Bullet Points

Thinking about the friend or family member you are focusing on in this section, make a list of three gifts and/or callings. Pray over the list. Bless those gifts and callings in the person. Then write a more detailed word for them that pertains to the items on your list. Next, go back to Day Twelve. Did any of your bullet points about this person match what you had written in your first word for them? How can the two words you wrote work together? Remember, we are not sharing these words.

Today's goal is to grow in getting words specific to an area in a persons life

"For by grace you have been saved through faith; and that not of yourselves, it is the gift of God."
Ephesians 2:8

"There's something about valuing people not because they value you, but because you can see God in them."
Kris Vallotton

Day Fifteen
Bullet Point/Prophetic Word Follow-Up

Using the word you journaled on Day Twelve and the bullet point list, today craft a word for your friend. A crafted word is a word that has been organized, prayed over, and written in a concise manor. Again, we are not yet delivering these words.

Today's goal is to adapt our journal words into easy to communicate, shorter words.

"And the peace of God, which surpasses all comprehension, will guard your hearts and your minds in Christ Jesus."
Philippians 4:7

"God doesn't call the equipped, son. God equips the called."
Rick Yancey

Day Sixteen
Question and Answer

Ask the Lord some questions about your friend. Are there areas He would like you to intercede? Maybe there are specific encounters you can declare? Ask for words of knowledge that could be useful the next time you see them that could turn the conversation towards Jesus without sounding religious. Journal what you hear, see, and feel. Document the ways in which the Lord asks you to steward what He has shown you.

Today's goal is to hear from God how we are to steward the words He gives to us.

"Yet those who wait for the LORD will gain new strength; they will mount up with wings like eagles, they will run and not get tired, they will walk and not become weary." Isaiah 40:31

"There is no better evangelist in the world than the Holy Spirit." Dwight L. Moody

Day Seventeen
Prophetic Sentence

Write out a one sentence prophetic word for your friend. Look for the word the Lord is highlighting. Ask God why that particular word is a key. Journal what the Lord is speaking to you about this highlighted word.

The goal of today's exercise is to continue to sharpen our attention to detail and learn how to process the details of what we see and hear.

"All Scripture is inspired by God and profitable for teaching, for reproof, for correction, for training in righteousness;"
2 Timothy 3:16

"Truth is a person who lives within His people. We are liberating Jesus, separating our old from our new so that we can walk in newness of life." Graham Cooke

Day Eighteen
Color and Draw

In today's entry we are drawing again. Ask Holy Spirit for a word for your friend, and then draw a picture that represents that word. Remember, it doesn't have to be perfect. It can be more about the colors or even abstract.

Today's goal is continuing to break down walls of how the Lord might speak to us and how different kinds of prophetic words might speak to people.

"By this all men will know that you are My disciples, if you have love for one another." John 13:35

"God is always advancing and looking for new territory to take you into. God doesn't play defense, He plays offense."
Bob Hazlett

Day Nineteen
Prophetic Dream

Today we are going to ask God to give us a dream we can declare for our friend. This exercise can work a few different ways. You can ask The Lord, "What is Your dream for my friend?" or "What is a dream my friends has?" Write them out, and then declare them. You could also write and declare a dream you have for them.

Today's goal is to partner with God to hear, see, and call out the deep desires of the heart for those around us.

Jesus answered, "I am the way and the truth and the life. No one comes to the Father except through me."
John 14:6

"You are never to old to set another goal or dream another dream." CS Lewis

Day Twenty
Prayer Journaling

The last nine days we have focused our journaling on a person. Journal about the overall experience of focusing your prophetic gift in a specific direction. Think about your interactions with the person over the last nine days. Have you seen a change in the person? Did your love and even your grace for that person increase? Maybe you have a testimony to document. if we don't share all the words we get, when we get them, lives are still affected by our partnership with the prophetic and our declarations

Today is about celebrating your progress

"So faith comes from hearing, and hearing by the word of Christ." Romans 10:17

"If we are followers of Christ, we are His disciples and should have the primary devotion in our lives to see as He does, think as He thinks, and understand with His heart." Rick Joyner

Day Twenty One
Freestyle

Over the next ten days, we will be focusing on a country. Today think of a country you love or are interested in, and then let your mind wander. After a bit of wandering, start writing. Once again we are starting with free write, so don't worry if what you write doesn't make sense now or seems to have nothing to do with your country. Free writing has a way of becoming something relevant.

Today's goal is to remind ourselves that prophetic journaling doesn't have to be labored; we know His voice.

"Surely the Lord GOD does nothing unless He reveals His secret counsel to His servants the prophets." Amos 3:7

"The destiny of the world rests upon the Church being able to properly say something, see something, so that the world can experience something." Larry Randolph

Day Twenty Two
Bullet Points or Lists

Read what you wrote yesterday. Pull out and make a list of the things the Lord highlights. Don't try to find reasons right now, just look for the highlights. Ask the Lord why He highlighted those words. How do they relate to your country?

Today's goal is to exercise our ability to recognize what The Lord is highlighting.

"With people this is impossible, but with God all things are possible." Matthew 19:26

"Do not pray for tasks equal to your powers. Pray for powers equal to your tasks." Phillips Brooks

Day Twenty Three
Color and Draw

Today we are back to drawing. Like you did on Day Nineteen, ask for a prophetic word, this time over your country. Then draw it.

Today's goal is prophesying from a different perspective and being creative.

"And He has filled him with the Spirit of God, in wisdom, in understanding and in knowledge and in all craftsmanship."
Exodus 35:31

"We are awakening to that marvelous truth, that Christ is not in the heavens only, nor the atmosphere only, but Christ is in you."
John G. Lake

Day Twenty Four
Prophetic Dream Interpretation

Think of the country you have been writing about. Maybe God has spoken to you before about this country. Has He placed dreams in your heart for this country in the past? If He has, recall that dream. As you journal, add any prophetic insight you receive along the way. If you haven't had a dream about your country, look up the vision, mission statement, or purpose for it becoming a country. Write a prophetic word that your country would step into the destiny they were created for.

Today's goal is to prophetically partner with Heaven for your country's call.

"Things which eye has not seen and ear has not heard, and which have not entered the heart of man, all that God has prepared for those who love Him." 1 Corinthians 2:9

"We want something fresh. We want revelation, not information." Leif Hetland

Day Twenty Five
Bullet Point Follow-Up

Look back over your bullet point list from Day Twenty Two, your drawing from Day Twenty Three, and yesterdays dream interpretation. Write a prophetic word that blends the three together.

Today's goal is to learn how different kinds of journaling can work together to form a strong word

"For the LORD God is a sun and shield; the LORD gives grace and glory; no good thing does He withhold]from those who walk uprightly." Psalm 84:11

"We are the decisive factor in the affairs of the universe."
Derek Prince

Day Twenty Six
Mind-Mapping

Write your country's name in a box in the center of the page. Ask Holy Spirit for words or short phrases that you can branch off. If any of your "branches" inspire you, write a short word for your country.

Today's goal is finding the things The Lord is doing in a country and its people.

"Therefore, brethren, be all the more diligent to make certain about His calling and choosing you; for as long as you practice these things, you will never stumble." 2 Peter 1:10-11

"Requests and petitions are the prayers of hope. Proclamation and declarations are the prayers of faith. Praise and worship are the prayers of love." John Crowder

Day Twenty Seven
Question and Answer.

Ask God some questions about your country, and record the answers. These can be details you have already seen about your country but want to know more about. It can be in regards to news stories or events you may have heard about, or you can ask Him to show you new things you did not know.

Today's goal is to exercise our gift and extend our faith in the area of hearing The Lord for the world.

*"Let the heavens be glad, and let the earth rejoice;
And let them say among the nations, 'The LORD reigns.'"*
1 Chronicles 16:31

"The clock in Heaven says 'it is now time to seek the Lord.'"
Banning Liebscher

Day Twenty Eight
SOAP Method
(Scripture, Observation, Application, Prayer)

This time you are going to pick out your own Bible verse. Pray and ask the Lord for a scripture to declare over your country. How does the passage apply and relate to your country? Is the context of the verse applicable to your country? Write a prophetic word that includes the promise of the scripture you chose for your country. How does the verse relate to past, current or future events.

Today's goal is to incorporate scripture into our prophetic words.

*"All nations whom You have made shall come and worship
before You, O Lord, and they shall glorify Your name."*
Psalm 86:9

"Time we spend with Jesus meditating on His Word and His majesty, and seeking His face establishes our fruitfulness in the kingdom." Charles Stanley

Day Twenty Nine
Prophetic Sentence

Write one prophetic sentence that you can memorize and declare over your country. Then ask God to highlight one of the words in your sentence. Ask for more understanding of this word, and journal what the Lord is speaking to you about the highlighted word.

Today's goal is sharpen our attention to detail and practice prophetic declaration over the world.

"But indeed, as I live, all the earth will be filled with the glory of the LORD." Numbers 14:21

"There is no greater gift than realizing the constant presence of the Divine and His Absolute Power to create and restore all things." Marta Mrotek

Day Thirty
The Last Day

You did it! You made it through thirty days of journaling. Today journal what prophesying over a country was like. Did it stir something in you for the nations? Did you grow in love for the people of that country? Read your entries from the last nine days, and do some investigation to find out if any of your words came to pass.

Next, take time to write about the experience overall. Now that you have written about a general topic, a person, and a country, do you feel Holy Spirit has shown you an area of influence? How do you feel about journaling overall? Will you continue to journal on your own?

Celebrate. Well done.

"He has told you, O man, what is good; and what does the Lord require of you but to do justice, to love kindness and to walk humbly with your God." Micah 6:8

"Prophecy is not a ministry skill, it is a life Skill."
Dan McCollam

ABOUT THE AUTHOR

Becky King is part of the prophetic community at The Mission Church in Vacaville CA. She is a dynamic speaker with a powerful gift of insight and an inspiring ability to take people through prophetic processing and identity. She is passionate about imparting and equipping believers around the globe.

Currently residing in Vacaville, CA. Becky is an Alaskan native who spent most of her growing up years in the Seattle area.

Made in the USA
Middletown, DE
22 June 2015